M000106106

IN RECITAL®
Duets
Volume One

ABOUT THE SERIES • A NOTE TO THE TEACHER

The *In Recital® Duets* series focuses on fabulous duet repertoire intended to motivate your students. All volumes of *In Recital®* address the issue of motivating students with attainable goals. The comprehensively leveled curriculum makes that possible, and this duet series offers a wonderful repertoire opportunity for your students. You will find original duets, duet arrangements of popular pieces, and duet arrangements of famous classical themes. There are equal-part duets as well as unequal-part duets that can be played by the teacher or a more advanced student. The duets in this series address a wide variety of different musical and technical issues, giving you the selection needed to accommodate your students' needs and plan recital repertoire for the entire year. The series provides practice tips, rehearsal suggestions, and duet performance strategies to help your students be successful!

 Use the enclosed CD as a teaching and motivational tool. Have your students listen to the recording and discuss interpretation with you! To learn how to use the CD as a valuable practice aid, turn to page 48.

THE FJH MUSIC COMPANY INC.
Frank J. Hackinson

Production: Frank J. Hackinson
Production Coordinator: Philip Groeber
Art Direction: Terpstra Design, San Francisco, in collaboration with Helen Marlais
Cover and Inside Illustrations: Keith Criss
Engraving: Tempo Music Press, Inc.
Printer: Tempo Music Press, Inc.

ISBN-13: 978-1-56939-519-6

ORGANIZATION OF THE SERIES
IN RECITAL® DUETS

The series is carefully leveled into the following six categories: Early Elementary, Elementary, Late Elementary, Early Intermediate, Intermediate, and Late Intermediate. Each of the works has been selected for its artistic as well as its pedagogical merit.

Book Five — Intermediate, reinforces the following concepts:

- More compound meters are used such as $\frac{9}{8}, \frac{12}{8}$.

- Students play syncopated rhythms and more complex sixteenth-note patterns.

- Students experience chords and their inversions, as well as chords and melody within the same hand.

- An introduction to syncopation and Ragtime, as well as Latin rhythms.

- Rolled chords.

- Mixed duplets and triplets in the same piece.

- Simple ornamentation.

- Modulation from one easy key to another easy key.

- A variety of major and minor keys.

THE BENEFITS OF PLAYING DUETS

Duets are good for a student's sense of rhythm and ensemble. They learn to "catch" the rhythm — whether it is fast or slow, and they learn to listen to each other and produce subtle changes in dynamics and tempo. Furthermore, playing duets gives students the opportunity to sense their partner's musicianship. The hands-on experience of interacting with another musician and enjoying each other's spirit in the music is an important step in developing their understanding of musicality. Duets can be an integral ingredient in lighting the musical fire!

An ensemble recital is great fun, and a mixed program of solos and duets provides variety for the audience. Playing duets for friends, family, other students, or for school is a wonderful way to spread the joy of music.

Enjoy all of these wonderful duets!

All but one of the pieces in this book are equal-part duets. *Maple Leaf Rag* is an unequal-part duet, with the *primo* part being slightly more difficult than the *secondo* part.

TABLE OF CONTENTS

Primo parts played by Helen Marlais; Secondo parts played by Christine Kim.

A Special Note to Students:

For centuries, people have played duets together. Without movies, television, or stereo, pianists of all ages would come together and play as a great source of entertainment. The most popular orchestral pieces, operas, and advanced piano works were often written for four-hands at one piano, called the "piano duet." This way everyone could enjoy the music of the day right at home!

This collection of duets is for you to play and enjoy! All of the duets are different in character, and each creates a different mood for you as well as for the audience!

Tips for Practicing at Home:

Here are a few practice suggestions for you to do at home. They will help you play these duets successfully with a partner:

1) Practice your part until you can play it without stopping (with correct notes and steady rhythm) before you go to your lesson.

2) Mark in specific starting locations throughout each duet to make your rehearsal easier and more effective. Start at these various locations when you practice at home so you will be ready for your rehearsal.

3) Listen to the CD recording so that you can hear the complete duet. In order to prepare well, listen to the tempo, rhythm, dynamics, articulations, and overall ensemble playing.

Tips for Practicing with your Duet Partner:

1) In order for the ensemble to work well and look professional, start with your hands in your lap. You and your partner should bring your hands up to the keyboard at the same time. Breathe together to begin the duet for perfect synchronization! (Don't count off.)

   After playing, both you and your partner should end with your hands in your lap. Then you are ready to stand and bow after the performance, which you should also practice together.

2) Decide with your ensemble partner who has the melody at any given moment. Ask yourselves, "Which part should be brought out over the other part?"

   After you have played the duet, ask yourselves, "What was the balance like between the melody and the accompaniment throughout the entire piece?"

3) While you are practicing, you might wish to count together; this way you'll be sure to play together at the same tempo and without stopping.

4) Poise at the piano — decide with your partner how you will walk on stage, stand at the piano, and bow to the audience. If you practice this often, you will be very polished at the performance!

5) Discuss with your partner which person can turn each page more easily and practice this well. This is one mark of true professionalism as a duet team. The more nodding and breathing you can do together, the more in sync your pieces will be. Nodding and breathing are good ways to synchronize your timing, just don't overdo it. It should not take attention away from the music. Instead, practice enough so that you can naturally feel each other's pulse and musical gestures.

6) If you have the opportunity to have a page-turner, practice nodding to indicate your page turns. You should not say anything or make any sound that takes the listener away from the music.

7) Really listen to your duet partner's part so you both play completely together.

   Above all, enjoy making music with another person! If you are having trouble with specific parts of the duets, practice more at home so you can concentrate on the musical aspects in rehearsal.

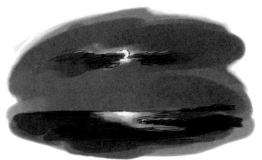

CLAIR DE LUNE

Secondo

Claude Debussy
arr. Timothy Brown

FJH161

CLAIR DE LUNE

Primo

Claude Debussy
arr. Timothy Brown

Secondo

Primo

GREENSLEEVES

Secondo

English Folk Song
arr. Melody Bober

FJH161

GREENSLEEVES

Primo

English Folk Song
arr. Melody Bober

Secondo

Primo

Secondo

Primo

Serenade

Secondo

Franz Schubert
arr. Edwin McLean

FJH1616

SERENADE

Primo

Franz Schubert
arr. Edwin McLean

Moderato (♩ = ca. 66)

H1614

Secondo

Primo

* Ornaments are optional.

CARNIVALE

Secondo

Valerie Roth Roubos

FJH1614

CARNIVALE

Primo

Valerie Roth Roubos

Latin style (♩ = ca. 104)

Secondo

Primo

Secondo

Primo

SWING LOW, SWEET CHARIOT

Secondo

Traditional Spiritual
arr. Kevin Olson

Gospel feel, with emotion (♩. = 100)

FJH1611

Swing Low, Sweet Chariot

Primo

Traditional Spiritual
arr. Kevin Olson

H1614

Secondo

I____ looked o - ver Jor - dan and

what did I see,____

A____ band____ of

an - gels a - com - in' af - ter me,____

FJH1C

Primo

Secondo

Primo

MAPLE LEAF RAG

Secondo

Scott Joplin
arr. Edwin McLean

Tempo di Marcia (♩ = ca. 138)

FJH1610

MAPLE LEAF RAG

Primo

Scott Joplin
arr. Edwin McLean

Tempo di Marcia (♩ = ca. 138)

Secondo

(Optional: D.C. al Fine)

34   FJH16

Primo

(Optional: D.C. al Fine)

OH! SUSANNA

Secondo

Stephen Collins Foster
arr. Timothy Brown

FJH16

OH! SUSANNA

Primo

Stephen Collins Foster
arr. Timothy Brown

H1614

Secondo

Primo

BOLERO

Secondo

David Karp

Tempo di bolero (♩ = ca. 116)

FJH16

BOLERO

Primo

David Karp

Tempo di bolero (♩ = ca. 116)

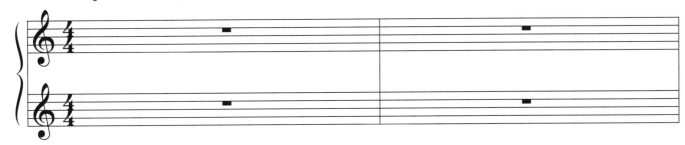

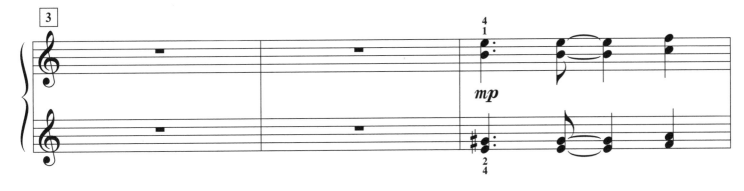

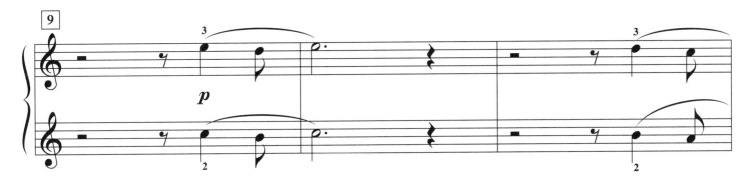

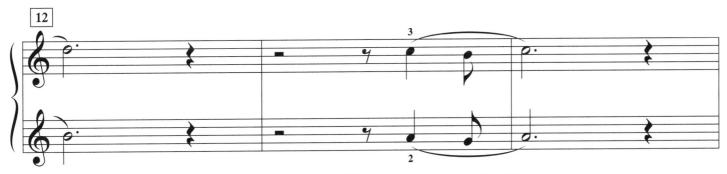

H1614

41

Secondo

Primo

Secondo

Primo

Melody Bober

Piano instructor, music teacher, composer, clinician—Melody Bober has been active in music education for over 25 years. As a composer, her goal is to create exciting and challenging pieces that are strong teaching tools to promote a lifelong love, understanding, and appreciation for music. Pedagogy, ear training, and musical expression are fundamentals of Melody's teaching, as well as fostering composition skills in her students.

Melody graduated with highest honors from the University of Illinois with a degree in music education, and later received a master's degree in piano performance. She maintains a large private studio, performs in numerous regional events, and conducts workshops across the country. She and her husband Jeff reside in Minnesota.

Timothy Brown

Timothy Brown holds a master's degree in piano performance from the University of North Texas, where he studied piano with Adam Wodnicki and music composition with Newel Kay Brown. He was later a recipient of a research fellowship from the Royal Holloway, University of London, where he performed postgraduate studies in music composition and orchestration, studying with English composer Brian Lock. His numerous credits as a composer include first prize at the Aliénor International Harpsichord Competition for his harpsichord solo *Suite Española* (Centaur Records). Mr. Brown leads a very active career as an exclusive composer and clinician for The FJH Music Company Inc.

Mr. Brown's works have been performed by concert artist Elaine Funaro on NPR, and most recently at the Spoleto Music Festival and the Library of Congress Concert Series in Washington D.C. His numerous commissions include a commission by *Clavier* Magazine for his piano solo *Once Upon a Time*, edited by Denes Agay. Mr. Brown is currently a fine arts specialist for the Dallas Public Schools and serves on the advisory board of the Booker T. Washington High School for the Performing and Visual Arts in Dallas, Texas.

David Karp

Dr. David Karp—nationally known pianist, composer, and educator—holds degrees from Manhattan School of Music and the University of Colorado. He has also done graduate work at Teachers College, Columbia University. Dr. Karp is currently professor of music at SMU's Meadows School of the Arts and director of the National Piano Teachers Institute.

As a clinician and adjudicator, Dr. Karp has traveled the United States from Alaska to New Hampshire, as well as internationally. He has been a guest conductor and commissioned composer for the New Hampshire Summer Piano Camp at Plymouth State University, and was recently honored with the establishment of the David Karp Piano Festival, which is held each spring at Kilgore College. In June 2002, Dr. Karp served on the panel of judges for the Van Cliburn International Piano Competition for Outstanding Amateurs.

Edwin McLean

Edwin McLean is a composer living in Chapel Hill, North Carolina. He is a graduate of the Yale School of Music, where he studied with Krzysztof Penderecki and Jacob Druckman. He also holds a master's degree in music theory and a bachelor's degree in piano performance from the University of Colorado.

Mr. McLean has been the recipient of several grants and awards: The MacDowell Colony, the John Work Award, the Woods Chandler Prize (Yale), Meet the Composer, Florida Arts Council, and many others. He has also won the Aliénor Composition Competition for his work *Sonata for Harpsichord*, published by The FJH Music Company Inc. and recorded by Elaine Funaro (*Into the Millennium*, Gasparo GSCD-331). His complete works for harpsichord are available on the Miami Bach Society recording, *Edwin McLean: Sonatas for 1, 2, and 3 Harpsichords*.

Since 1979, Edwin McLean has arranged the music of some of today's best-known recording artists. Currently, he is senior editor for The FJH Music Company Inc.

Kevin Olson

Kevin Olson is an active pianist, composer, and member of the piano faculty at Utah State University, where he teaches piano literature, pedagogy, and accompanying courses. In addition to his collegiate teaching responsibilities, Kevin directs the Utah State Youth Conservatory, which provides weekly group and private piano instruction to more than 200 pre-college, community students. The National Association of Schools of Music has recently recognized the Utah State Youth Conservatory as a model for pre-college piano instruction programs. Before teaching at Utah State, he was on the faculty at Elmhurst College near Chicago and Humboldt State University in northern California.

A native of Utah, Kevin began composing at age five. When he was twelve, his composition, *An American Trainride*, received the Overall First Prize at the 1983 National PTA Convention at Albuquerque, New Mexico. Since then he has been a Composer in Residence at the National Conference on Piano Pedagogy, and has written music commissioned and performed by groups such as the American Piano Quartet, Chicago a cappella, the Rich Matteson Jazz Festival, and several piano teacher associations around the country. He holds a Doctor of Education degree fron National-Louis University, and a bachelor's and a master's degree in music composition from Brigham Young University.

Kevin maintains a large piano studio, teaching students of a variety of ages and abilities. Many of the needs of his own piano students have inspired more than 100 books and solos published by The FJH Music Company, which he joined as a writer in 1994

Valerie Roth Roubos

Valerie Roth Roubos earned degrees in music theory, composition, and flute performance from the University of Wyoming.

Ms. Roubos maintains a studio in her home in Spokane, Washington, where she teaches flute, piano, and composition. She is active as a performer, adjudicator, lecturer, and accompanist. She has lectured on various topics and taught master classes at the Washington State Music Teachers Conference, Holy Names Music Camp, and the Spokane and Tri-Cities chapters of WSMTA. Ms. Roubos has played an active role in the Spokane Music Teachers Association and the Washington State Music Teachers Association.

In 2001, the South Dakota Music Teachers Association selected her as Composer of the Year and with MTNA commissioned her to write *An American Portrait: Scenes from the Great Plains* published by The FJH Music Company, Inc.

Ms. Roubos was chosen to be the 2004 – 2005 Composer in Residence at Washington State University. The Washington State Music Teachers Association selected her as the 2006 Composer of the Year. Ms. Roubos' teaching philosophy and compositions reflect her belief that all students, from elementary to advanced, are capable of musical playing that incorporates sensitivity and expression. Her compositions represent a variety of musical styles, including sacred, choral, and educational piano works.

USING THE CD

A great way to prepare for your duet performances is to use the CD in the following ways:

1) Listen to the complete performances of all the pieces. In this way, you will understand the different styles and personalities of each of the pieces. Enjoy listening to these duets anywhere, anytime! Listen to them casually (as background music) or attentively. After you have listened to the CD, you might discuss interpretation with your teacher and follow along with your score as you listen.

About the *primo* and *secondo* parts: (These Italian music terms are pronounced "PREE-moh" and "seh-KOHN-doh")

Remember that the *primo* part is always on the right-hand side of the book, while the *secondo* part is always on the left-hand side of the book. The *primo* part usually stays above middle C, while the *secondo* part usually stays below middle C.

2) The CD can also be used as a practice partner, because you can play along with the performances.

Playing along with the performance track encourages flexibility in rhythm and musicality, because the pianists are playing as if in a performance and not with the metronome. This is exactly what will occur when you are performing with a duet partner. Be sure that you practice your duet part by itself, with the metronome, before you attempt to play along with the performance track and before you rehearse with your partner.

48

FJH16